DISNEY
FROZEN

Level 2

T0346075

Re-told by: Hawys Morgan
Series Editor: Rachel Wilson

Before You Read

In This Book

Queen Elsa

Princess Anna

Olaf the Snowman

Activity

Read and say True or False.

1 There is a frozen castle in the mountains.
2 It is sunny and hot in the mountains.
3 There is ice and snow in the mountains. It is cold.

Elsa and Anna are sisters. They live with their parents in a beautiful castle. It's in Arendelle. Elsa can make snow with her hands.

They make a snowman. Anna laughs,
"Catch me!" She is running quickly on the snow.
Elsa says, "Slow down!"

Suddenly, Elsa's ice hits Anna.
She's weak and cold. Elsa holds Anna
in her arms and says, "I'm sorry!"

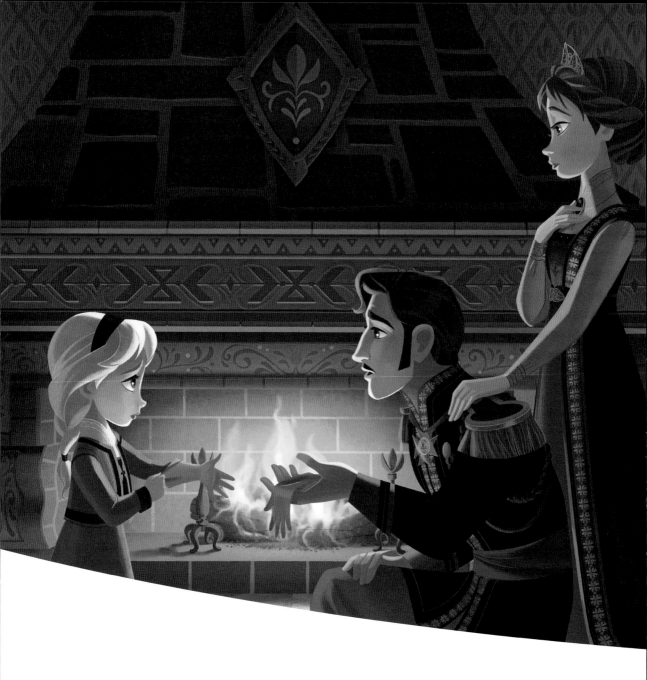

Anna is okay, but Elsa is scared.
Her magic snow and ice are dangerous.
Their parents close the castle doors.

Every day, Elsa sits in her room. Anna asks her to play, but Elsa says, "Go away!"

Anna is a young woman now and Elsa
is Queen of Arendelle! Anna is happy.
The castle doors are open again.

That night, Elsa and Anna fight.
Elsa is angry. Suddenly, magic ice flies from
her hands and it freezes Arendelle.

Elsa thinks she is dangerous. She runs
away. The water freezes under her feet.
Anna follows Elsa, "Stop!" she says.

Elsa makes a blizzard of ice and snow.
She's happy! Her magic isn't dangerous here
in the mountains.

Anna meets Kristoff and a magic snowman, Olaf. They help Anna find Elsa in the mountains.

Anna asks Elsa to melt the ice.
Elsa says she can't. "Go home, Anna!"
Magic ice flies and hits Anna's heart.

Then Elsa makes a big snowman. Anna,
Kristoff, and Olaf are scared. They run quickly
down the mountain to Arendelle.

Anna is freezing. There's ice in her heart.
Who can help her?
Then Elsa arrives and holds her frozen sister.

Elsa cries. She loves her sister. The ice melts,
Anna is warm. Elsa opens the castle doors again.

After You Read

1 **What happens first, second, and third?**

2 **Read and match.**

1 He is a magic snowman.
2 She can make snow and ice.
3 He helps Anna in the blizzard.
4 She is frozen.

3 **Read and say Anna or Elsa.**

1 "Catch me!"   **3** "Go away!"
2 "Slow down!"   **4** "Stop!"

Picture Dictionary

angry

dangerous

freeze

hold

ice

magic

melt

mountain

scared

warm

weak

Phonics

Say the sounds. Read the words.

S s

sister

snow

Z z

blizzard

frozen

Say the rhyme.

A frozen snowman is having fun,
Olaf sings, "I love the sun!"
Freezing blizzards, ice, and snow,
Sisters sing, "Let it go!"

Values

Say sorry.

Find Out

What can you see at the Snow Festival in Japan?

Before the festival, snow arrives in trucks. Then they make big snow sculptures. There are sculptures of animals, buildings, and famous people. People visit the festival and have fun in the snow! After the festival, they take the snow away.

snow sculpture

Who is this?

Pearson Education Limited
KAO Two
KAO Park, Harlow,
Essex, CMI7 9NA, England
and Associated Companies throughout the world.

ISBN: 978-1-2923-4671-7

This edition first published by Pearson Education Ltd 2020

7 9 10 8 6

Set in Heinemann Roman Special, 19pt/28pt
Printed by Neografia, Slovakia

Published by Pearson Education Limited

Acknowledgments
123RF.com: madllen 18
Getty Images: The Asahi Shimbun 21
Shutterstock.com: anochastock 21, kyslynskahal 18, Leonid Ikan 16, retirementbonus 20, Sean Xu 17, Sebastian Duda 17

For a complete list of the titles available in the Pearson English Readers series, visit www.pearsonenglishreaders.com.

Alternatively, write to your local Pearson Education office or to Pearson English Readers Marketing Department, Pearson Education, KAO Two, KAO Park, Harlow, Essex, CMI7 9NA